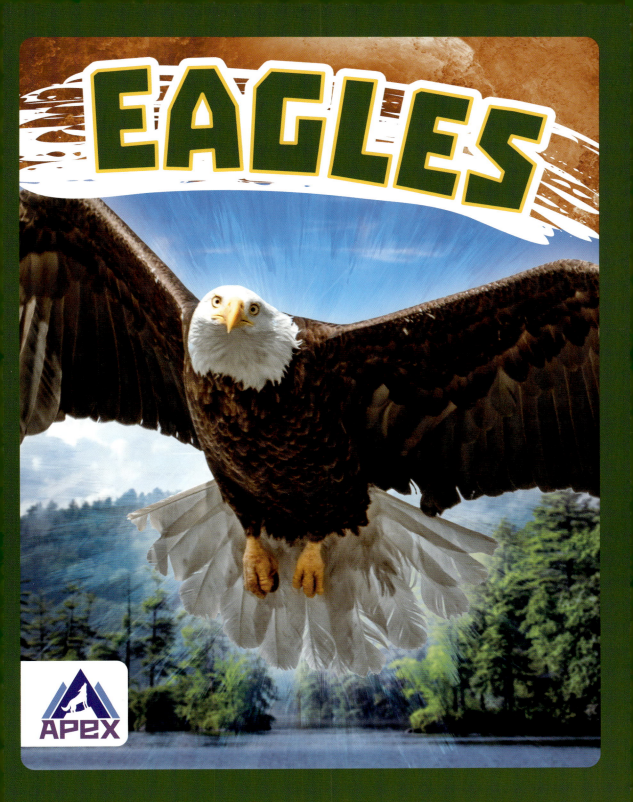
EAGLES

By Golriz Golkar

WWW.APEXEDITIONS.COM

Copyright © 2022 by Apex Editions, Mendota Heights, MN 55120. All rights reserved. No part of this book may be reproduced or utilized in any form or by any means without written permission from the publisher.

Apex is distributed by North Star Editions:
sales@northstareditions.com | 888-417-0195

Produced for Apex by Red Line Editorial.

Photographs ©: Shutterstock Images, cover (bird), 1 (bird), 4–5, 6–7, 8–9, 10–11, 12–13, 13, 14–15, 16–17, 18–19, 20, 21, 22–23, 24–25, 26, 27, 29; Unsplash, cover (background), 1 (background)

Library of Congress Control Number: 2021915652

ISBN
978-1-63738-141-0 (hardcover)
978-1-63738-177-9 (paperback)
978-1-63738-248-6 (ebook pdf)
978-1-63738-213-4 (hosted ebook)

Printed in the United States of America
Mankato, MN
012022

NOTE TO PARENTS AND EDUCATORS

Apex books are designed to build literacy skills in striving readers. Exciting, high-interest content attracts and holds readers' attention. The text is carefully leveled to allow students to achieve success quickly. Additional features, such as bolded glossary words for difficult terms, help build comprehension.

TABLE OF CONTENTS

CHAPTER 1

A FISH DINNER 5

CHAPTER 2

AN EAGLE'S LIFE 11

CHAPTER 3

FLYING HIGH 17

CHAPTER 4

HUNTING FOR PREY 23

Comprehension Questions • 28

Glossary • 30

To Learn More • 31

About the Author • 31

Index • 32

CHAPTER 1

A FISH DINNER

A bald eagle **soars** high in the sky. The bird spots a salmon swimming in a river. The eagle spreads its powerful wings. It swoops down toward the water.

Bald eagles often live near rivers, lakes, and oceans.

The eagle grabs the salmon with its **talons**. Small bumps on the talons help the bird grip the slippery fish.

SYMBOLS OF STRENGTH

Eagles are fast and strong. As a result, people often use them as **symbols** of power. For example, eagles appear on many coins and flags.

Eagles can snatch fish right out of the water.

The eagle flies back to its nest. It shares the fish with its babies. It rips pieces of meat with its sharp beak.

Eagles build nests high up in trees or on cliffs.

Eagles build huge nests. Some golden eagle nests are 10 feet (3 m) wide!

CHAPTER 2

AN EAGLE'S LIFE

There are more than 60 types of eagles. Some live near water. Others live in forests, **prairies**, or deserts.

Steppe eagles live in grasslands and dry areas.

Steller's sea eagles live on the coast of eastern Russia. They often fly south in the winter.

Some eagles migrate. They travel to find food or warmer weather. Other eagles stay in the same area for their whole lives.

ENDANGERED EAGLES

Harpy eagles live in rain forests. But people cut down many trees in these areas. Many eagles have lost their homes. They are beginning to die out.

Harpy eagles live in Asia and South America.

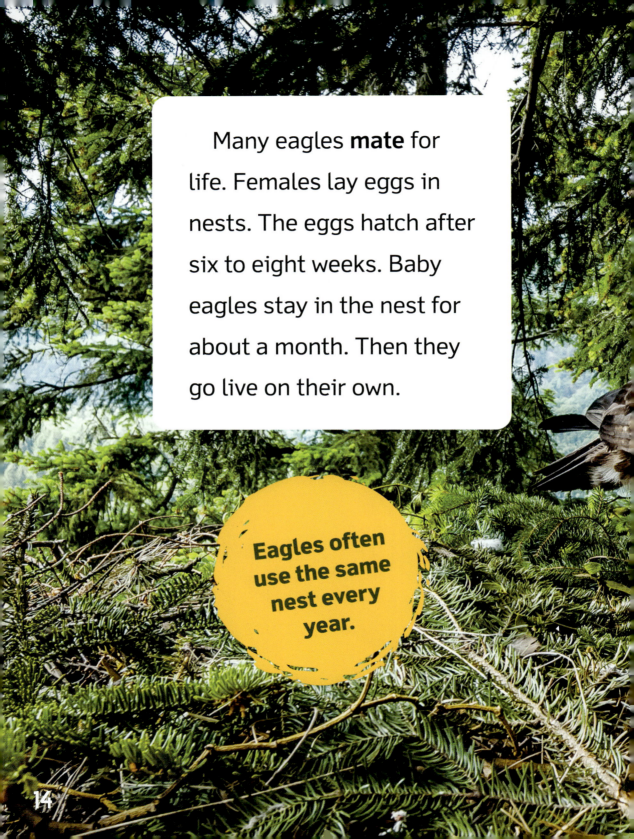

Many eagles **mate** for life. Females lay eggs in nests. The eggs hatch after six to eight weeks. Baby eagles stay in the nest for about a month. Then they go live on their own.

Eagles often use the same nest every year.

CHAPTER 3
FLYING HIGH

Eagles come in a variety of colors and sizes. Many eagles grow nearly 30 inches (76 cm) tall. Their wings can stretch twice as wide.

A golden eagle's wings can be more than 7 feet (2 m) wide.

When soaring, eagles catch currents of air. The moving air keeps them high in the sky.

Large wings help eagles soar. By not flapping their wings often, the birds save energy.

Female eagles are often much bigger than males.

Eagles have excellent eyesight. They can see **prey** from far away. And they can fly very fast to catch it.

Tawny eagles often fly down from trees to catch prey.

Harpy eagles are large birds. They can weigh up to 20 pounds (9 kg).

A harpy eagle has a crest of feathers on its head. The eagle can fan out these feathers to scare away threats.

EAGLE SPEEDS

Eagles soar at about 30 miles per hour (48 km/h). While diving after prey, they go much faster. Some go more than 100 miles per hour (161 km/h).

CHAPTER 4
HUNTING FOR PREY

Most eagles eat small **mammals**. Some eagles catch fish and snakes, too. Large eagles may even hunt monkeys or deer.

Eagles often eat rabbits and other small animals.

Eagles reach out with their feet to grab prey.

Eagles catch prey with their large talons. Eagles have four talons on each foot. Their grip can be 10 times as strong as a person's.

A harpy eagle's talons can be 5 inches (13 cm) long. That's bigger than a bear's claws!

Eagles' hooked beaks are razor-sharp. Eagles use their beaks to tear food. Eagles even eat animal bones.

With their sharp beaks and claws, wedge-tailed eagles can hunt animals as big as kangaroos.

Bald eagles often find or take prey that other animals have already killed.

SOMETIMES SCAVENGERS

Some types of eagles can be **scavengers**. They eat the remains of dead animals. Bald eagles and golden eagles are two examples. Eagles may even steal food from other animals.

COMPREHENSION QUESTIONS

Write your answers on a separate piece of paper.

1. Write a few sentences describing how eagles hunt their prey.

2. Which kind of eagle would you most like to see in real life? Why?

3. Which body part does an eagle use to grab its prey?

   A. its long wings
   B. its large beak
   C. its sharp talons

4. What could happen to harpy eagles if people keep cutting down trees in the rain forest?

   A. The eagles could die out completely.
   B. The eagles could have more space to live.
   C. The eagles could find and eat more food.

5. What does **migrate** mean in this book?

*Some eagles **migrate**. They travel to find food or warmer weather.*

- **A.** to move from one place to another
- **B.** to stay in the same place
- **C.** to become a different animal

6. What does **remains** mean in this book?

*Some types of eagles can be scavengers. They eat the **remains** of dead animals.*

- **A.** living things
- **B.** large areas
- **C.** leftover parts

Answer key on page 32.

GLOSSARY

crest
A tuft of feathers or skin that sticks up.

mammals
Animals that have hair and produce milk for their young.

mate
To form a pair and come together to have babies.

prairies
Large areas of land covered in tall grasses.

prey
An animal that is hunted and eaten by another animal.

scavengers
Animals that eat dead animals they did not kill.

soars
Flies high in the air without flapping wings very often.

symbols
Objects or ideas that stand for and remind people of something else.

talons
Long, sharp claws that birds use to hunt.

threats
Things that are likely to cause danger or harm.

TO LEARN MORE

BOOKS

Hamilton, S. L. *Eagles.* Minneapolis: Abdo Publishing, 2018.

Lawrence, Ellen. *Harpy Eagle.* New York: Science Slam!, 2020.

Sommer, Nathan. *Golden Eagle vs. Great Horned Owl.* Minneapolis: Bellwether Media, 2021.

ONLINE RESOURCES

Visit **www.apexeditions.com** to find links and resources related to this title.

ABOUT THE AUTHOR

Golriz Golkar is a former elementary school teacher. She has written more than 40 nonfiction books for children. She loves to sing and spend time with her daughter.

INDEX

B
bald eagles, 5, 27
beaks, 9, 26

D
deserts, 11

E
eggs, 14

F
fish, 6, 9, 23
food, 12, 26–27
forests, 11, 13

G
golden eagles, 9, 27

H
harpy eagles, 13, 21, 25

M
migrating, 12

N
nests, 9, 14

P
prairies, 11
prey, 20–21, 25

S
salmon, 5–6
scavengers, 27
soaring, 5, 19, 21

T
talons, 6, 25

W
wings, 5, 17, 19

Answer Key:
1. Answers will vary; **2.** Answers will vary; **3.** C; **4.** A; **5.** A; **6.** C